Darwin's Garden

Darwin's Garden

*studies from life
by Lee Rossi*

- 2019 -

Darwin's Garden
© Copyright 2019 Lee Rossi
All rights reserved. No part of this book may be used or reproduced in any manner whatsoever without written permission from either the author or the publisher, except in the case of credited epigraphs or brief quotations embedded in articles or reviews.

Editor-in-chief
Eric Morago

Associate Editor
Michael Miller

Marketing Specialist
Ellen Webre

Proofreaders
Jim Hoggatt & José Enrique Medina

Front cover art
"The Dream" by Henri Rousseau

Back cover photo
Arthur Rothstein

Book design
Michael Wada

Moon Tide logo design
Abraham Gomez

Darwin's Garden
is published by Moon Tide Press

Moon Tide Press #166
6745 Washington Ave. Whittier, CA 90601
www.moontidepress.com

FIRST EDITION
Printed in the United States of America

ISBN # 978-0-9974837-8-9

To my family, and to the whole human family

Contents

Foreword by Michael Diebert 8
By Way of Introduction 11

Votive

Adam's Bastard 14
Out of Naples 15
A Habit of Ascent 17
Original Sin 19
Spraying for Pests 20
Two Acres and a Lawn Mower 21
Sudden Harvest 23
Chicken Pox 25
Straight Edge 26
Fish on Friday 27
Poison 28
Taps 30
Increase + Multiply 31
It Smells Like Alcohol 32
Figure Drawing 33
Hay Ride 35
Clinkers 37
Lasting Things 38

Rebel with a Thousand Causes

Coat of Arms 42
Stoicism for the Masses 43
Prodigal (Parable of the Traffic Stop) 44
Mother Tongue 46
Missouri Roll 47
Last Stand 48
Knucks 50
To The Blackout of '69, Ithaca, New York 52
Ole Folks 54
A Naked Thumb 56
A Good White-Collar Job 58
Smoke Bomb 60

Poker Party	62
Parable of the Mules	64
Goin' to the Dogs	66
"What a Bringdown"	68
The N-Word	70
An Attic in Downstate Illinois	71
Anywhere but Mississippi!	73
Crapheads	75
Pastures	78
Rockets' Red Glare	80

Lucky Stiff

The Aerialist	84
Gare Saint-Lazare	86
Foil	87
Liebestoadstool	88
April's Fool	90
Horizon Event	91
Lip Service	93
Ludus Amatorius (The Sport of Love)*	95
Nocturne: Crow and Weasel	97
Naked	99
Kumquat	102
Undergrowth	103
A Tour of Scotland: An Epithalamium	104
Confessions of a Lapsed Gym Rat	105
Dinner with the Cannibal	106
Forty	107
A Field	109
Family Tree	111
Hallein Above Salzburg	112
Wasserspiele	114
Draining the Lake	115
Seahorse in Saw Grass	117
Amandatory	119
About the Author	120
Acknowledgements	121

Foreword

In *Darwin's Garden*, Lee Rossi is obsessed with his past, and in turn, *the* past: who are we, and what is the through-line from then to now? But he also explores how the past makes the present (and, in turn, the future) possible. These poems provide plenty of imagistic and tonal reminders that the garden, that seductive, lush paradise, was probably always a fiction. Yet we persist in believing we can recapture it—and perhaps, in fleeting moments, we manage to.

"Out of Naples" sets the lament: the garden as both a place forever lost and a place where we long to return. Rossi, though, smartly avoids nostalgia by emphasizing that his freshly exiled ancestors also want to return here yet will never arrive:

> Trading towers of true stone for towers
> of rebar and concrete, they set out
> from sluggish, crowded ports on boats
> listing, febrile with rust.
>
> They left their mothers' dark shawls
> and dresses, which hid the only
> goodness they had ever known.
>
> Now they would taste life's bitterness
> in every cup, in every crust of bread.
> Better off, some thought, to have been born dead. (5-14)

Exiled from the garden, we quest for a new garden. But like Rossi's forebears, we are likely to find an unruly wilderness populated with other seekers: "the sprawling / fields, the swamps and unruly forests, / the strangers speaking a Babel they barely / understood, ghost-haired or pelted like animals / insistent, capricious, voices like wind / or water rushing over rock and sand" (17-22). What to do? Like us, they have "armed themselves with hatred and regret / ... dispensing / their world wisdom from behind a glass / of grappa in a dusty village square" (23-28).

Yet *Darwin's Garden* also acknowledges that the elusive dream, even when seemingly achieved, is fraught with its own menaces: chemicals ("Spraying for Pests," "Poison"); burning coal ("Clinkers"); mean dogs and speeding cars ("Rockets' Red Glare"); and racism and provincialism ("Chicken Pox," "Taps," "Parable of the Mules"). And several poems simply doubt our readiness to inherit the dream and its attendant responsibilities. In "A Good White-Collar Job" and "Poker Party," the teenaged boys studying for the priesthood are conversant in languages other than the one they're studying for: "We didn't have a calling – / even if that's what they called it – / leaping at truth / like trout to the lure" ("Good" 1-4).

    For all their carefully mapped anxieties, though, these poems are not despondent. The final section insists on the continual search for beauty and "lasting things"—not as a cure-all, but as a way of staying sane. The voices are conciliatory, even hopeful that the past can be learned from and improved upon in the present. The finely tuned "Draining the Lake" is Larkin-esque in its deft exploration. In an ancient city (the perfect place to dig up the past), the speaker recalls the energy of a long-ago romance in the presence of his long-ago lover:

> I remembered her, still almost a girl,
> lithe as exposed wire, electrons ready to jump
> into my hand and burn through my body.
> Who had she become, who once was so hungry for love? (13-16)

The kinetic energy of the past is then imprinted on the poem's present, in lakes resembling "the chambers of a heart, pumping the valley's / blood into the river…" (21-22) and ducks which "guided their little families in tight formation, / like convoys on the lookout for U-boats" (26-27). Here it might be easy for the romantic to slide into the bathetic or bombastic. Instead, the romantic is joined by the trenchant pragmatist:

> I could almost see myself on the bottom of the lake,
> slowly decomposing, but alert enough
> to notice the oddly matched couple staring
> at the surface. Maybe we'd always been wrong
> for one another. How could anyone understand
> my habit of going in the wrong direction?
> I seemed immune to the usual sorts of happiness.
> I seemed to thrive on mistakes.
> How else explain how happy I'd become? (36-44)

From the bottom of the lake to happiness in nine lines—the speaker is in a different sort of Eden, one carved from experience but especially from learning. For us wanderers, this may be a much more achievable (and advisable) goal. If Darwin is already in the garden—if he was there all along, in fact—maybe *Darwin's Garden* is a wake-up call: keep evolving.

—Michael Diebert
Author of *Life Outside the Set*

By Way of Introduction

In *Fever Pitch,* his memoir of life as a British soccer fanatic, Nick Hornby observes, "The white south of England middle-class Englishman and woman is the most rootless creature on earth; we would rather belong to any other community in the world. Yorkshiremen, Lancastrians, Scots, the Irish, blacks, the rich, the poor, even Americans and Australians have something they can sit in pubs and bars and weep about . . . but we have nothing, or at least nothing we want." I suppose a middle-class Catholic boy from the suburbs of St. Louis might feel something similar. Two generations away from Italy, six from Ireland and France, I had nothing of that volatile mix of cultures which I could call mine. I was simply American, white as Wonder Bread, bland as apple sauce. The melting pot had taken my ancestors, their many shades of red, brown, and blond and out popped me, gently pink, with smudges for eyebrows and hair. In the meantime, all that was unique and troubling about the Irish, the Italians, or the French peasantry was elided, a sooty residue of ambition and resentment that colored everything.

VOTIVE

Everything else you grow out of, but you never recover from childhood.

— *Beryl Bainbridge*

Adam's Bastard

After Adam made his break—who could blame him for tiring of perfection—he began to tire of his mate. If she wasn't sweating all that stooping and gathering, she was constantly apologizing. He had his own regrets and didn't need hers as well. It slowed his reflexes, made him thoughtful, timid, clumsy. Either hit the sabretooth smack in the ribs or watch your javelin sail into an impenetrable thicket. One day he came across tracks he'd never seen before, some five-toed, bipedal creature had been walking near the lakeshore in an inch of volcanic rain. Hefting his club—strong enough to crack the skull of any megatherium or glyptodon—he set out after his two-footed prey. It didn't take long to run her down, a small, shambling ape-like creature, who despite her hair and limited vocabulary reminded him of someone, not himself of course, but maybe his talkative, long-suffering mate. He liked it that she didn't say much and that he didn't need to waste a lot of effort getting her attention. He liked her direct friendly way. He imagined it had something to do with his superior height, his large muscles. She kept touching his pale skin as if she couldn't understand why he was so naked. So, he let her live, and subsequently sought her out, although after the day's hunt, he always returned to Eve. Once or twice he even shared his kill with the creature. He called her Lucy, or maybe that's what she called herself—in his old age he could barely remember. And the baby? It had his face, but her skin, her sturdy load-bearing gait. He named it after her—Lucifer. Of course.

Out of Naples

The land, its poverty concealed
by olive groves and fields of grape.
Cypresses rose like tongues of fire
in the gently astringent wind.

Trading towers of true stone for towers
of rebar and concrete, they set out
from sluggish, crowded ports on boats
listing, febrile with rust.

They left their mothers' dark shawls
and dresses, which hid the only
goodness they had ever known.

Now they would taste life's bitterness
in every cup, in every crust of bread.
Better off, some thought, to have been born dead.

* * *

Wherever the boats took them,
others of their kind were already there,
the dark cities and slums, the sprawling
fields, the swamps and unruly forests,

the strangers speaking a Babel they barely
understood, ghost-haired or pelted like animals,
insistent, capricious, voices like wind
or water rushing over rock and sand.

They armed themselves with hatred and regret
vowing to return when luck favored
them, they would be great men,

clad in pesos and dollars, dispensing
their world wisdom from behind a glass
of grappa in a dusty village square.

* * *

They slept for decades, dreaming
that they slaughtered cattle, flayed corpses,
dug ditches, lashed rope to spar and mast,
brewed whiskey and sold it,

murdered or married
when they had to, fathered children,
whimsical, disdainful, blonde,
creatures as shy as rabbits,

and when they woke, they were dying,
surrounded by angelic hosts,
blonde strangers who smiled on them

as they had seen the Madonna smile
when as children they knelt at her altar
to pray and light a votive.

A Habit of Ascent

Childhood, the first eternity,
as I wandered our vast acre,
trying to escape the sun.

How lonely it seemed with no children
nearby, just my sister, an insistent mouth
at Mother's worried breast.

Catalpa trees fanned their leaves like aunts
trying to save their powder from streaking.
No clambering into their narrow laps.

The pear oozed like a teenager
craggy with acne, its bark a magnet
for columns of ants.

I circled the firs and stroked the knees of elm and oak,
giants in conversation
as the wind riffled their hair.

Only the apple tree
was short and broad
enough to harbor this restless climber.

Its cool fire surrounded me
as I climbed into flowered lace
and huddled in the second crook, watching

leaves, then apples, sweeten on stems,
here where the trouble all began,
in the garden of the heart.

At night, I dreamed
the whole miracle again,
an explosion of green branching into darkness,

and yet I wanted more,
some escape from what I was,
from what my parents wanted me to be.

Come morning I'd drape myself along a limb
like a python, inhale the husky perfume, stroke
the swollen fruit, as if this had always been my home.

Original Sin

I did not know my illness
even when I knew its name,
its symptoms, its synonyms—

cancer, totalitarianism, the avant-garde,
fast-food, social networks.
It belonged to someone else.

That's what I thought. How could something
so vast have anything to do
with me? If I had had parents,

they would have explained why
I was sick, but my parents suffered
the same disease. Both fled

the farm when they were too young
to see what was driving them away—
the bankers, the tractors, prejudice and erosion,

metal birds picking at the rocks—
wealth for someone, but not for them.
Eden, it was someone else's Eden—

their purgatory, or worse. Listen,
I don't excuse them. They refused
to understand what they already knew,

the killing and everyday cruelty,
which was someone else's life, but
thank God, not theirs.

How can I excuse myself?

Spraying for Pests

Silver tank strapped to his back
my father might have been a space-walker
or scuba diver trawling
the deeper reaches of a reef.

The bottles he poured wore
the Jolly Roger. They grinned
at my sister and me from their high perch
in the fruit cellar, above rows

of mason jars filled (not with fetal
monsters à la the Natural History Museum)
but canned peaches and pears.
Feet splayed and crouching

under his burden, he trundled
from tree to forbidden tree,
waving the wand like a fairy
blessing all with poison mist.

Winter long we dined
on swollen, unblemished fruit,
juices sweet as the tropics,
ripe as the unborn.

Two Acres and a Lawn Mower

He would've mortgaged his soul
for that spread of suburban green—
or she would've. As it was, they promised
the bank thirty years hard labor

mixing drinks and cutting hair,
the same indenture
their neighbors served.
Free to go to work, free to fall

into bed at the end of 12-and
14-hour days. And then, one day
off, not a day of rest exactly,
the day when everything else

got done, the grass higher
than ankles, fruit placidly rotting
in the shade. He'd take the oil
can and the gas can outside,

measure the oil, pour it into
the gas, cap it, slosh it, spill
it into the mower, which would
never start, which bucked

and coughed like somebody's
consumptive grandpa before
belching to life, spouting smoke
and leaf litter before hurling rocks

in all ten directions of dismay,
sharper than shins, wicked on ankles.
Nothing could stop him once it started,
his genie, his team of Missouri mules,

he was only there to follow it
and watch the green harvest,
a shower of blades burdening
the thick canvas bag. As helpless

as a child, or a man with wife
and children to support, he
followed its desecrated path—
a monk on the way to nirvana.

Sudden Harvest

One August bagworms lit my father's
evergreens like Christmas lights, thousands
of gold cocoons. Simple materials,
needles and something like spit
to hold them together. He told me
to get outside and pick them off the bushes.
I see myself standing there hesitant,
a tin pan dangling in my hand.

What was I thinking? The nuns at school
were always reminding us of the pains
of hell, the fire, the darkness, the worms
that ate but did not consume the sinner.
Or maybe I was thinking about Aunt Marge
in her beautiful cherry box,
cushioned by velvet on all sides.
The worms would be halfway through
the wood by now. In less than a year
there'd be nothing but holes.

When my father came out to cut the grass,
he yelled at me, I remember that,
above the roar of the mower,
so I started, the heat like a fur coat
turned inside out, the sweet smell
of clipped grass, the choking smoke.
The pods were sticky, prickly.
As I worked I saw the inchlings
crawling from their sleeping bags
like kids waking at camp.

When the pan was full, he took it
and told me to come with him out back
to the trash pit where we burned
newspaper. I loved watching
each sheet as it blackened, curled,
and revealed the unburnt page beneath
just before it caught. But not this time

when he poured my little captives
onto the charred ground,
shook gas onto them—
I thought of the priest at High Mass
sprinkling us with holy water—
and lit them like charcoal.

Oh, they curled too in the sudden heat,
blood-smoke rising sideways in the pit.
What must he have thought, seeing me
staring, fists clenched, the moisture
boiling from my cheeks and eyes,
trying to read that fiery script?

Chicken Pox

Six days in my darkened room—
twice as long as Jesus—
silent as meat in a meat locker,
as a corpse in a morgue,

the only human sound my mother
like the attendant at an old folks home
or the nurse in an asylum, shuffling
in and out with a gruel of vanilla

ice cream melting in 7-Up—
her all-purpose remedy.
Nothing to do but listen to voices
on the radio—Lone Ranger and Tonto

(baritone and tenor)—the ricochet
of bullets carving faces in the action—men
hunched over microphones, heavy-hoofed
men clomping wooden squares—

echo-filled spaces where a bed-ridden
boy might wander, its only hero.
But what about those others—
Holy Mack'rell dere, Andy—

always scheming—you could hear it
in his blustery basso—that Kingfish!—
not a bad guy maybe, just the kind who'd take your car,
your dad's car for the afternoon—

Check and double check!—learning then
what the white man's burden might be,
when the day came for me
to pick up my gun and be one.

Straight Edge

Imagine a ruler of infinite length
marked in centuries and millennia,

anchored at zero, and ending tonight,
this minute, this instant.

I'm lying in bed, a crucifix wrapped
in papery palm on the wall above my head.

A mute beast, its cosmic chill circles
the house looking for a way in—

I am the traitor who leaves the gate
unlatched, the emptiness of history,

the vacuum of time pouring in
like the Great Flood, four thousand and

four years before this new era, the one
that leads inevitably to this moment.

Somewhere nearby my parents snore and stir
unaware that the enemy has breached their walls,

my sister sleeps dreamless in her cocoon.
Only I know the evil that will destroy us,

have traced its footsteps back
past the dunking stools, the pillories and guillotines,

past the flails and barrels of pitch,
iron maidens, racks and armories,

blades, pikes, singing and sweating blood.
When was the age ever not dark?

Fish on Friday

The air above the chicken-wire shack filled with smoke
and the smell of carbon, the pop and sizzle
of milky flesh in tanks of molten grease.

Flickers dove into the trees. Blue eyes black in the deep shade,
my parents sat at a picnic table hoarding their bottles,
sipping the sweaty ones and whispering like waves in retreat.

Bored with ourselves, my sister and I caught
fireflies and squashed them with our hands.
The gravel driveway glistered like a road after summer rain.

I chased her through tall grass, a hungry bass
eager to swallow a smaller fish.
Nickel-sized bites swelled on my ankles.

At school, we learned how Jesus had called
Simon and his brother Andrew
from their nets and made them fishers of men.

I could see Jesus walking on top of the waves,
schools of small children nibbling his feet,
and Peter swallowed by a whale as he floundered.

And I could see my family swimming
in ignorance and sin,
how we were suddenly scooped from cool waters

and thrown, gasping, into the bottom
of a boat that smelled of tar and blood—
salvation carrying us to a farther shore.

We ate and ran off, only the tops of trees still in light,
the muggy air thick enough to swim,
my sister and I flailing our arms, trying for land.

Poison

We were pals   even though I hated
    his outhouse, even though I coveted
        his BB gun,
knocking squirrels   and robins
    out of the elms around his house.

His folks had an ice box,   not a fridge,
    the ice on top keeping things cool,
        and a washing
machine churning   on the porch,
    a wringer for sluicing wet clothes.

He let me use the gun,
    but I just wasted his ammo,
        like years later
at the shooting range   with my girlfriend
    and her father. I was useless,

hitting 3 out of 50.
    She hit 8 or maybe it was 10.
        Every time I looked
over my shoulder   my future father-in-law
    just shook his head. I never shot anything

except my sister, but that was after talking
    my parents into buying me
        a pump-action
Daisy, not the Winchester lever-action model
    but the kind where the pressure built.

I was aiming wide right, but managed
    to shoot her in the arm.
        My mom didn't think
anything of it. You could see   where the BB hit,
    all red and swollen,

but it was just a BB, and mom didn't
    see a hole. But we were out back,
        that pal of mine,
playing burn out,   trying to break
    one another's glove hand with a fast ball,

and getting thirsty.   We could've gone inside
    but he saw the can my father used
        to spray the fruit trees.
You put water in it and something called pesticide,
    twisted the top shut and pumped.
We could have gone inside, but no,   he said
    we could just drink from the can.
        so he started
pumping and offered me the wand.
    "You first," he said, and when

after drinking some,   I handed it back,
    he just laughed and said, "Not me,
        that stuff's poison."
A week after I shot her, they took my sister
    to the ER and dug a BB out of her arm.

Taps

That Sunday our parents abandoned
Ed Sullivan and the June Taylor hoofers

to watch us tap-dancing Indians
on stage at the local Catholic school.

In khaki buckskins and red felt fringe
we shuffled and stamped like bison in tall grass.

We shook our home-made headbands, crow
feathers dipping and swirling above our heads.

The boards of our tiny reservation resounded
like the struck bars of a xylophone.

Our pale faces shone with mascara & rouge.
What did we know of Indians

except what flickered on imagination's screen,
frenzied dramas of provocation and revenge?

Shod with metal, we traded gun fire
until the whole audience, those innocents,

swooned, wounded with parental love.
We danced, the very image of their dreams,

savage flesh clothed in music and time.

Increase + Multiply

Like actors waiting to audition, our 5th grade class
leaned against windows and black boards.
None of us knew our lines. I stared at the drizzle outside,
and the woods beyond the cemetery. "***Three times nine.***"
Mrs. Shepherd, the teacher, fed us our cues.
Harry Gerken, always the fool, sat down first.
Anna Ozga could've been queen, but drowned
in "***four times four's***" shallow water. David and Fred,
would-be killers who get murdered in the wings,
both missed "***six times twelve.***" "*Seventy-two*," I piped
like a tenor singing the musical interlude. Maureen
provided comic relief with her impression of a clam.
Then Billy, expert tragedian, fell on his sword.

I looked at the far wall, empty now of children,
our history projects on low tables beside the teacher's
desk. I'd built a California mission with every piece
of Block City I owned, a squat rectangular nave,
two towers hung with Christmas bells.
No roof, as if it had collapsed in a temblor.
No tannery, no fields, no dormitories for the priests,
the Indian men, the women. No soldiers.
So much was missing. I didn't know what.

Soon it was just Sharon and Dale and me.
There was only one lead in this play. "***Seven times eight.***"
I was sure Sharon knew the answer, but stage fright got her.
She was wearing the same glasses as the teacher.
She was looking at the teacher's unwieldy, pregnant
stomach. "***Seventy-eight***," she said, and I smiled.
Dale and I traded answers like street punks
fighting over a girl. When we got to the 12's,
he slowed, stumbled, and I leapt in for the kill.
I had the role, Chief Know-Um-Tables.
Anxious to mount the stage, ready for a life
of adulation, I went back to my seat.

It Smells Like Alcohol

or the inside of trees.
I use it like a soldering gun
to weld the sheets of plastic,

almost weightless parts—
aileron, stabilizers and fin,
fuselage and cowling—

gray as metal melted at the joins,
the bitter taste on my tongue—
spirit that drives metal through air,

buoyant and unseen—
fused into violent sculpture,
the oblique instruments of my father's

survival—Wildcat and Hellcat,
Mustang, Lancer and Thunderbolt,
Liberator, Marauder and Superfortress—

I arrange them on shelves above the desk,
the blotting paper blued with dark glue scars,
these angels of my delivery, seeming

to circle in some darkened fly space,
a celestial holding pattern.
I turn bas relief into three dimensions,

praying for Time to make a fourth,
the one in which I disappear.

Figure Drawing

The art teacher—she was just
    someone's grandma—
but what did the nuns,
    that murder of crows

(pale hands, pale faces
    poking from their habits),
what did they know
    of beauty?

The un-nun said it was simply
    a matter of proportion—
the legs, the arms, the torso,
    all multiples of the head.

Increase the multiple you got
    a super-model,
lessen it you got a dwarf.
    I was a patient child

with a talent for numbers,
    as careful as a girl,
so I got it right, in the same way
    I got my other lessons right.

It looked even less real
    than my sister's cardboard dolls,
the ones she cut from books
    and draped with two-dimensional

clothes, pink and green party dresses,
    to cover the pink skin and white
underwear. What I wanted
    was a view of the swelling

under bra and panties,
    what made it painful
to be a girl. I remembered the doll
    at the museum of natural history,

a Paleo-Indian, naked except
    for a necklace of claws and
the savage ornament at her crotch.
    I took my drawing

home, and drew mounds
    on the chest, hair where the legs
came together. There was mystery
    there and I wanted to touch it.

Hay Ride

There is a rightness to the cruelty
    of children, an exactness that cuts
        away what is unnecessary

in other children. Boys will steal
    your innocence, girls rip
        your gentleness. Why

should you enjoy the comforts
    of childhood, when they have
        thrown theirs away? The wagon

bounced and shuddered along
    the rutted river bottom trail,
        boys and girls jostled into

boards and one another, skin
    prickling with hay-borne
        itch. The smell of cows in the barn,

the smell of manure lingered
    in nostrils. The damp
        twilight air sweated

a brooding mist over the fields.
    I had nothing to say to the others.
        That was my way, keeping my

distance. Impossible in that heap
    of teenagers. I pushed a girl away,
        below the waist, knowing about

levers and centers of gravity,
    about fulcrum and force.
        She flew off the back end.

And when she scrambled back,
    she taunted me, accusing me
        of touching her

in an unforgiveable place,
    a place only she could touch.
        What did I know, who was

only beginning to learn
    the ways of cruelty and desire?

Clinkers

Just as I believed in fire, I believed in hell.
Late September a truck parked in the side yard
and thrust its conveyor into our basement window—
a flying filling station nursing a Stratofortress—

emptying itself into the coal bin,
a small dirty room gleaming now with anthracite.
Soon as the weather got cold, I'd dip a filthy bucket
into that Mesozoic stream and pour it

into the hopper's green maw, never appeasing
its insect voracity—so like my own digestion—
mineral orts fed the furnace, its great silver body,
arms upraised like the priest at Consecration.

Next morning I'd be back to pry
the furnace door as gingerly as if I were spying
on my parents in bed, recoiling from the heat
and grappling with a long-handled claw

like a physicist fumbling with plutonium.
Slowly I lowered unconsumed rock and metal,
glowing like a meteor fresh from its ride through the atmosphere,
into a ten-gallon lard can. What was I wresting from the flames

and dragging to the slag heap behind our house?
Was I some angel plucking the misbehaved but repentant
from Purgatory's cleansing fires,
or some minor demon hauling the remains

of a truant life after the purified soul
ascends to its reward?
Or was I merely witness to a life consumed
by everyday oxygen, the soul spent

on its own diurnal pleasures and pain,
nothing left of all those thoughts and prayers,
that bickering and occasional kindness,
nothing of my small, replaceable life but the husk?

Lasting Things

Like a whistle only dogs can hear
or notes tuned to adolescent ears,

like bats swooping through invisible night
with only uncanny sonar to guide

their dim-sighted way, like supersonic
angels ablaze at wave lengths hidden

to everyone but God, these inhabitants
of a world not quite ours pass

stealthily, like minutes and hours,
impervious to every sense but dread.

We call them many things, ancestors,
forebears, the loving dead,

but can never quite escape the sting
of their regard, their disappointment

and perpetual jealousy. Only when we join them
in their contempt for the living

do we understand, finally, what they mean,
those quaint concepts, eternity and hell.

REBEL WITH A THOUSAND CAUSES

I will not serve that in which I no longer believe whether it call itself my home, my fatherland or my church: and I will try to express myself in some mode of life or art as freely as I can and as wholly as I can, using as my defense the only arms I allow myself to use—silence, exile, cunning.

— *James Joyce*

Coat of Arms

A length of rusty galvanized,
pretzeled like the Gordian Knot,
gules on a field of *vair.*

A bright green garden snake
chopped in four with a hoe
on a field of concrete.

A red and white checkerboard,
like the tablecloth
in Italian restaurants.

Three rings, one gold,
one figured with lilies, the last
triple twisted—

all three interlaced
like links of chain mail
on an azure field.

This is my escutcheon,
its charges and tinctures,
its stains properly furred—

and from restless-hearted Faust—
das ewig Weibliche—
the motto of the house.

Stoicism for the Masses

Who needed money when all you had to spend it on
were indulgences or the wishbone of a saint?

We were always trying to wake into summer
even during winter's slush and chapped melancholy.

In a world filled with false appositives, suffering
was the only synonym, a knotted cord, a beauty mask

of ashes and spit. We're crouching beneath trees, hiding
in canebrakes, sprawled in pools of water, wishing

that the thunder of cavalry were just thunder.
It's the thirteenth century and people are expert

at dying. We've studied tauntology—bravery
being nothing more than stepping from behind a shield

and meeting the enemy's spear with your chest.
In six hundred years, the descendants of our cruel

and merciless lord will crush organized labor
cruelly and without mercy. A century on

they'll marry us, thankful for their partners' rugged energy,
complement to their own nifty education and sense of style.

But for the moment thorn birds sing cheerily, hidden
in blackberry thickets, and children tie one

another to trees. They're playing heretic and inquisitor,
the rest of us cheering the warmth of an imaginary fire.

Prodigal (Parable of the Traffic Stop)

It wasn't much of a town,
one stop sign and a row
of store fronts, all of them
closed that time of night.
But it had a traffic cop and
traffic court, and when they
added up the violations
(running the sign, reckless
endangerment, failing to
halt, driving while under
the influence), they wanted
more than he had in his
pockets, more than the car
was worth. Nothing to do
but sit all night in their cell
and wait for *babbo*
to bail him out. It didn't help
he was what he was, not
anyone they'd meet at church
or say hello to on the street.
It was just one night—
and then it wasn't. What
happened to his pop,
where was the money
from home? A week went
by, a week in the fields,
and then another week
on a road gang. "Six months
hard labor," is what the judge
told him, the next time
in court. He was a white man,
what was he doing chopping
and cropping with the coloreds?
It wasn't fair. That's what he
learned, life isn't fair.
And six months in jail
in Southern Illinois, six months
lasts eight or maybe ten.

He got out, but had to hitch-
hike. The car, his car, belonged
to the town. And the roll of ones
wrapped with a twenty—
it had paid for his food.
But what about *babbo*?
Strangers disappeared
along that road all the time.
The women, wife and sister,
were sure the old man was dead,
shot in some barroom fight.
At least they got back the boy.

Mother Tongue

*(An Italian-American soldier guards internees
on the trip from Oakland to Crystal City, Texas)*

In the half light of the second-class car,
the faces of jostled sleepers gleamed like mushrooms
in the leafy undergrowth of their clothes.
He remembered the sour smell of mold
and fish guts along the muddy banks
of the Wolf River, his line taut in the cold
brightly wrinkled flood. He didn't know about
the other camps, six thousand miles away,
"factories of death." Sometimes he worried
that the prisoners would give him trouble.
The little kids were worst.
He was used to dealing with trouble
in small doses, a glass-jawed middleweight
with a good right cross or some cocky recruit
who knew too many slurs for Italians.
Nobody likes a fight. Not even fighters.
He patted his Smith and Wesson
as another small-town smear of light glazed
the windows. As a boy, he'd seen bloody-
aproned butchers put a gun to a cow's
temple, watched the muzzle explode,
blood rivering from mouth and nose.
He knew how savage those Southern boys could be,
and yet he was glad that *nono* had left
the old country, glad he was not dying
for *la patria* on some dusty hill.
All day the bronze train flowed past switching
yards and naked buttes rusting in the sun—
the cruelest landscape he had ever seen—
swallowed it, reducing it to nothing.
He tried to forget his own skin
darkening in the muggy fields back home,
tried to forget his mother's pale lips
mouthing the language of the enemy.

Missouri Roll

Whenever Dad walked into a new saloon,
he'd flash a wad thick enough
to choke the big-mouth bass
leering over the bar like a row
of gargoyles, passing judgment
on the drunks below. A roll of ones
wrapped in the thin blanket of a 20
and snugged with a burly rubber band.
What was he thinking? That the locals
would be impressed? He kept another roll,
of pennies, in his pants' pocket, the poor man's
brass knuckles—grip it in your fist
and slam it into someone's gut,
no broken bones and lots of extra
force. He'd been a boxer, 21 pro fights.
Maybe he missed the excitement
of the ring, the managers and cut men,
the hysterical, drunken crowd,
and needed some of that excitement
now that his life was just trays
of food and booze leaving
the kitchen and coming back empty.

But someone got wise to him.
He was only a welterweight
and could flatten the biggest guy
in the place. After a couple of beers
the barkeep slipped something into
his Schlitz—knock out drops—
and when he woke in the alley
behind the bar, his cash was gone,
the pennies too, and over all his body,
bruises bloomed like roses.

Last Stand

Beside the juke box, Custer, down
to his last men, stands tall in a field

of prairie grass, the rock of European
civilization assaulted by wave after wave

of native fury. Where is my father,
the man who died fighting

his own battle with the world,
damage and destruction

the surest way of knowing he's alive?
Was it Iwo or Guadalcanal,

was it the Bulge? Or was it
some back-alley brawl, fists no match

for knives, knife unequal to guns?
The woman at the bar will not say.

"Your father was a hero," is all she'll say,
a hero without picture or name.

Rows of bottles, fat and skinny, tall or squat
stand in tiers above the bar,

morning's glare caught
in their hopeful, unlined faces.

"Very handsome and very brave,"
is how she describes him,

as if he were the blonde and bearded West
Point graduate, last in his class, Civil War veteran,

brash, ambitious publicity hound,
lousy tactician, the hammer

to Reno's anvil, his force eradicated
in the time "it takes a hungry man to eat a meal."

A revolving diorama lights the back wall,
a mountain stream cascading

from frozen white to surging blue, and back.

Knucks

Late morning—fairway,
water hazard and green
steam like saunas.

I wait with the other caddies
beneath the trees—
parasitic growth,
a colony of mushrooms—

playing cards. I learn
a new game, like rummy,
but with penalties, a rite of
passage into the world of men—

lose and you cut the cards,
the winner doling out pain,
one stroke for each pip,
ten for Queen, Jack or King—

a short chopping motion
on the loser's knuckles—
like planing wood with a hatchet
or felling a small tree.

Once, having won,
I lifted my hand above the shoulder,
pretending a terrible strike—
only to tap my opponent twice lightly

and incur the maximum penalty—
a rule I hadn't learned or remembered—
fifty-two strokes for each violation,
a full deck of pain.

My Mother wants to know why
the backs of my hands
are bloody, the skin shredded.

My Father wants to know
why I let them do it.

What can I say? The pain is no
worse than the heat or trying
to breathe the water-logged air,
no worse than the nuns with
their rulers, no worse than her
hair brush or his belt.

I hold my hands beneath the tap,
groping for the future.

To The Blackout of '69, Ithaca, New York

*I think my father longed to disappear
While driving through this place once.*

    — Larry Levis

Driving along the highway I notice
cotton spilling from its bolls,
its secret night over, like a girl who suddenly removes
a scarf to wear her hair like a crown.

Once when I was seven,
my father drove along this same road—
my mother slept beside him and I was in back—
while his thoughts gathered overhead like a storm front
from the south and he was seized by a fierceness
he kept like the roll of pennies in his pants pocket.
He could've disappeared into the dark soil
of the river bottom. It took everything he had,
sweating and gripping the wheel harder,
to keep the left tires riding the center stripe.

What was it brought this on,
the road, the cotton, the sky
foaming to a frenzy?
I never knew.
When I left home, I wanted nothing that belonged to him,
not his bluster, not his acceptance
of pain, hard work, drunkenness and loss.

Now I can sit in my own car
and watch the fields turn to houses,
watch the stars pale and go out
in the glare of truck stops and malls.
I have kept silent for years,
amazed at my talent for suffering,
the way a tree will go on feeding the insects
which cause its death. And I have been the insect,
feeding on love until it too was dead.

I remember once, in a library,
after another day listening to my thoughts,
the lights went out, and though I'd been alone for hours,
the sudden darkness reminded me how vulnerable we are.
The silence surrounded me and swallowed
all the voices on all those shelves,
and I knew I would never have anything to say
that could out-shout death.

So I sat there, looking out my high window
like a sailor in a crow's nest, and saw the darkened valley
swell to definition in the moonlight, and at its center,
a lake carved by glaciers, passing on its twice-stolen light.
It was pity, then, I felt for the authors, and for my father,
who never wrote a letter that lasted more than three embarrassed lines.

I thought of his boxing, all the years of his adolescence,
the fact that he won
because he was willing to suffer more than the other guy.
And I remembered him driving that road fifty years ago,
eyes fixed on the white lines
as if they were an opponent's glove reshaping his face
with each jab, jab, jab.

And then the bell rang.
And then he was free to consider the woman sleeping beside him,
the child in the back seat staring at him
with eyes so like his own,
eyes that deepened into a lake splintered from a mountain of ice.

Ole Folks

Let's not talk about the small purgatory
of recess, the heat, the grass stains
and skinned knees, the third-graders

knuckle-walking through a forest
of wee six-year-olds,
let's ignore the endless wait

to climb the one slide's narrow
stairs, angels in ascent, devils
in the sandy pit at the bottom,

the same eternity waiting for a
wooden plank to lift me
closer to the empyrean

and quicker still dropping me
back to the fallen world—
all that practice for the boundless

punishment of death.
Nor have I anything good to say
about the nun, Sister Most Dear,

the steel rod of her eye brows
stretching from ear to ear.
She loved us, no doubt, as only

the forsaken can, she tortured us
with all the love she had for our ignorance
and willingness to obey.

If she gave anything, it was her
own thwarted love of music,
meter of discipline, every day

as we stood and sang from our song books,
this black-eyed immigrant girl
teaching us scales and modes,

teaching us to read by sight
whole, half and quarter notes.
Oh, she loved those melodies,

not just Gregorian but Stephen
Foster, his Jim Crow anthems
her very favorite.

We were her darkies, the school her plantation.
How we longed for the ruler and the slap,
our inheritance of murder and rape.

Only God could know us, our forgotten
sins, the sins committed by others,
for which we'd pay with this life and the next.

A Naked Thumb

There was just one league for junior bowlers,
Saturday morning, and anyone could join,

the small, the ugly, the uncoordinated,
kids whose idea of sport was "mutant."

But who wanted a plastic trophy for league
champions, high game, high three-game series,

anyway? Not the ambitious twelve-year-old,
me, or the owner's son, or his partner's

two kids—one of them a girl!—
it wasn't enough. We were chafing

to beat the adults at our game,
piled into those awful plastic chairs

behind the stacks of balls,
gazing enviously at the light-filled

precincts of gutter and alley,
as we watched the slaking of adult thirst,

listened to the buzz of adult chatter,
the rumble and lightning crack

at the end of the lane. We were
better than any of them, except for

the owner's other son—
soon to be transported to TV heaven, Chris

Schenkel's partner on the weekly pro broadcast—
Billy Welu, Don Carter, Dick Weber—

names as holy as the litany of saints—
he rubbed shoulders with them,

discussing the fine points we were still polishing.
Who knew, we were still getting better,

each to his own alley after school
almost every afternoon.

We hated those pins
almost as much as we hated our lives.

We wanted to knock them off their perfect perch,
those smug stoic bodies, erect as sailors

manning the rails or office seekers
at a Wall Street cocktail party.

We wanted to smash their imbecile serenity,
bury them in a mass grave.

So there we were, massaging our knees,
tending our carefully manicured thumbs.

Oh, how they failed us, our teenage skin
not thick enough for the professional

game, always calloused or forming blisters,
fissured like Lake Mojave. Don't tell me about warts!

We were a band of amateur dermatologists,
comparing symptoms and treatments,

olive oil, mom's expensive face cream,
stuff that smelled like airplane glue—

hell, it was airplane glue!—
anything to keep that fatal flap of skin

from shredding, anything to get us
monsters of ambition through the next game,

the only thing between us
and glory our naked thumb!

A Good White-Collar Job

We didn't have a calling—
even if that's what they called it—
leaping at truth
like trout to the lure.

We were nothing
special—going to class,
going to chapel,
content with the rain of insects
pimpling the water's skin.

We wanted to be priests
like the priest in our parish,
the friendly fellow who said mass
and drove a new Buick every
year, who heard confessions
and preached the building fund
until the church and school were paid for.

We studied basketball
and Latin and said the words
without quite understanding them.

We wanted away from our parents,
asleep over supper,
the brothers we slept with,
the sisters who tormented our dreams.

We rode the bus two hours
each way, the shuttle of our passage
weaving a garment of regret,
black and habitual.

We were readying ourselves
for a life of poverty (but not
too much), of chastity, but the
greatest of these is obedience.

The priests who
said their prayers kneeling
at the feet of teenage boys—

we told the bishop, and went
back to our books. We were going
to be clerks and quartermasters
in God's war of attrition
with the world.

Smoke Bomb

I was a refugee from the Little Ice Age
so, of course, these children of ease
found me odd and even a little frightening.

For them it was just "enrichment,"
something to do with their endless summer.
For me it was my life—

not just Catholic, but a seminarian,
I took their course in Freud and Marx,
heard their devoted recitations of Nietzsche,

and set them aside, offering discussions
of Aquinas and "natural law."
They had "class" and I had

the Great Chain of Being.
We were all just teenagers,
planning our escape from parents,

those unremarkable foundations
for our soon-to-be spectacular lives,
so we tested our strength, each

against every. They'd already outlived guilt,
the substance in which I swam,
as familiar to me as air to them.

How else explain the Great Famine,
the Plague and Hundred Years' War?
If they wanted comfort and suburbs far

from poverty, then millions had to die.
I didn't know that then, only that they
disliked me, wearing my ignorance

like a hair shirt. Once, coming back
from the bathroom I saw a group staring
at the parking lot, and looking out I noticed

two classmates bent over a car, my parents' car.
Maybe the hood was up, I don't remember,
but I hurried from that room, leather

briefcase heavy in my hand.
There was no one near the car.
The two I'd seen had vanished.

Surely, I was imagining it all. Why would
anyone harm me? I wasn't important
enough to be anyone's target,

but still I lifted the hood, clumsily, unsure
what I was looking for, never having
seen or even dreamed such mischief,

but there, attached to the engine, something
that didn't belong, a red tube.
I yanked it off, half expecting it to explode

in my hand, and threw it into the grass.
Back in class, I sat in self-imposed
quarantine, knowing now I'd been singled out

for punishment, knowing that it was God's plan
for me, a pariah, chosen to bear his load
of thousand-year-old books.

Poker Party

Half a dozen seminarians,
future bureaucrats of the Lord—
we tried so hard to be adult,
smoking, drinking somebody's parents' beer.
Pitiful. That useless wad of flesh tucked
snugly in our underpants. Seventeen-
years-old and never kissed a girl—
although some of us dreamed it.
Some of us dreamed of kissing a boy.

Poker's no good if you're not playing
for money, for blood. Sucking on
cigarettes, giving our cigarettes a blowjob.
We played for chips, for points.
Pointless.

Bored, we'd jump into some dad's Buick
and cruise the park, looking for fags
outside the men's john, or slide
past a long line of cars,
fog steaming windows,
fog of lust, fog of need.
We needed something to do
Saturday night, no girls in sight.
We'd sworn off girls for life,
our spiritual life—
a bunch of teenagers going crazy,
prosthetic hearts banging like a cheap drum kit
inside the smoke-filled darkness of our chests.

Sometimes we'd kill the lights
and slip behind a car,
then flip them on, shouting,
"God sees you," as we roared by.
Stupid. Plain stupid.
Trying to outrun some jerk with a hard-on.
I was a total jerk-off. We all were.

I'll stop now. I can see I'm boring you.
But that was the point. The boredom.
You've got youth gushing from all your spigots
like beer at a sodality mixer,
and you just turn it off!
And everybody's smiling
and gritting their teeth
and saying what a good thing you're doing
giving your life to God,
fucking up your life,
and meanwhile everybody else
is jumping into the bushes with one another
and getting something, you'll never know what,
how good it is.

They're laughing their asses off. At you.
And you're a dumb skull, you even believe
you're giving your life to something
higher.

And then you don't.

Parable of the Mules

We were walking past the corral, when all a sudden, my uncle says,
"It ain't right." There was a stallion in the corral, my uncle called it
'the paddock,' and the stallion was showing off. It was hot, hotter
than I was used to. Cotton was ready and the pond was green
with scum. Most of the time I'd been there, a couple of weeks
during summer vacation, he was just an old horse, but today
he was a stallion. I could hear the mares on the other side
of the barn sounding nervous. "What ain't right?" I asked.
"Mis-ceg-e-nation," he says, almost spelling it out. I was what,
I was eleven or twelve, and still had a lot to learn,
but I figured he wasn't talkin', or just talkin', about a horse.
"You know what I'm talkin' about," he says, so I nodded
and hoped that whatever it was, he'd just drop it.
But of course, I wouldn't be telling this story, if he had.
"Them nigras," he said, using a word that because I was
from up north, made me nervous, "it's really their fault.
A white boy can start going with a colored gal,
and pretty soon—they're miscegenating."
Now I was pretty ignorant, but I knew that that
wasn't what people usually called it. "You're almost grown,"
he said, "and pretty soon you'll want to be going out
with girls." Not me, I thought, but didn't know how to say that.
"So you stay away from them colored gals," he said.
But before I could even ask why, or begin to suggest
that maybe there might not be anything wrong
with dating someone from another race, he said,
"It's like horses—horses and zebras. Horses
and zebras don't mix. Horses is domestic animals
and zebras is wild, and there's always something wrong
with the offspring." I didn't know what to say, of course.
What I didn't know could've filled an NFL playbook.
Maybe when I studied biology. At any rate, I figured this
was an important piece of my education, something I'd
want to come back to and chew on from time to time,
but by then we were back of the barn where he kept
his prize mules. They were big, big as horses, and black.
and he warned me not to go near them, no carrots,

no sugar lumps, not even a pat on the nose. "They're mean, them mules, but they'll plow a field when it's too hard or too hot for a horse." I'm not sure whether the mules appreciated that kind of praise—they just stood there and didn't make a sound.

Goin' to the Dogs

I was under age—
which is to say *illegal*—
wearin' a broad-brimmed hat
my uncle gave me and sneakin'
into the dog races
over in West Memphis—
what was legal there but illegal
on our side of the river
where instead of racin' dogs
they fought their dogs to the death,
which was also illegal
but more fun
because watchin' somethin' die
is always more fun than just watchin' it lose—
of course, most everything was illegal
on the Memphis side of the river,
everything except 3.2 beer
which even the babies drank out of their nipple bottles
to keep 'em happy and put 'em to sleep—
Jim and Jack—you could buy 'em
every day but Sunday—no drinkin'
on the Lord's Day 'cept in your own house,
which was not illegal but contrary to the spirit of the thing,
none of the bars was open, so you'd have to go to a rib joint
or restaurant and pack your own
except if you knew the owner
and slipped him somethin',
you could get somethin' decent to drink.
Seeing we was Italian—
which was almost illegal
in the eyes of everyone includin' ourselves—
we wanted vino but settled for whiskey,
cuz back then nobody down there sold vino—
only the dagoes drank vino and there weren't enough of us
and besides we wanted to fit in.
So I snuck into the race track behind
my blue-eyed dad and my dark-skinned uncle,
me in the white Stetson pretendin'

I'm a baby-faced gambler,
and watched the dogs chase a metal rabbit
like I was watchin' the hare chasin' that tortoise
cuz they never caught up and never caught on—
studyin' what the adults was drinkin'—
beer for the women, whiskey for the men—
and how they'd tear up
them pink and blue tickets
after every race
like it was New Year's Eve.

"What a Bringdown"

Water in a fountain doesn't get me very high.

— *Ginger Baker*

One night only, rain sifting like seed pearls
from clouds of cotton batting, psychedelic
harbingers played the Auditorium.

War-wounded yet never been to war,
I hobbled on crutches past security, drunk
on young girls' beauty, their dresses billowing

about their knees like surf. The opening act played
one song five times, different keys, different speeds.
We were all young then, flaunting our long hair

and beards, floating like smoke
above ourselves, as union negotiations
between spirit and body kept breaking down.

Six-foot amps squatted atop one another like demon
acrobats endowed with chiliastic fervor, as if the millennium
could come and go during each six-minute song.

The bass thundered in clusters of sixteenth notes,
carpet bombing the audience.
We felt flayed and remade every second.

"Choose," we were told, "war and death,
or the disgrace of jail." We wanted a middle way,
and I chose mutilation, the surgeon's blade

excising a kneecap, small body part
unnecessary for all but kneeling in foxholes
or at the altar of authority.

Drugged on codeine and aspirin, I slumped in my seat,
my leg in its plaster cast thrust into the aisle
like a rudder vainly steering my little boat

through history's engulfing sea,
never sure of my destination—
innocence or complicity.

The N-Word

My tall, mocha-latte painter friend
waves her arms as if sketching
a new composition,

one that features a large oval
slashed by her hand's
terrible swift palette knife.

"I don't care what black people
do," she's saying, the cords
of her neck drawn tight

like halyards on the middle passage.
"I don't like when they say it
either, but it's unforgivable

when somebody white uses that word."
"What about," I'm about to ask
her if I could use it

to talk about my parent's racism,
all the slurs for all the groups
I learned at the dinner table,

when she cuts me off.
"If I heard a white person
say that word, I don't care

the context, I'd never speak
to them again." My skin
flushes umber, the word from

Umbria, whose poverty my grandparents
fled a century ago, or terra cotta,
for the earth we're all made of,

baked by prejudice. I take another
bitter sip of Chianti.

An Attic in Downstate Illinois

Even now there are places where a thought might grow.

  —Derek Mahon

For sixty years my mother's inheritance has languished here,
passed down from her father and grandfather,
in the house on the rise in a thicket of pine and skeletal elm,
the house that once had view of barn and stable and lake below the hill
and patchwork fields and forest stretching into the next county,
and later the woods thinning and dividing until there were only fields
and the lake shrinking, the grime of its retreat in concentric rings,
a salt depression now seeding the wind with dust,
and meantime giant iron birds piercing the crust, sucking oil from the deep rocks,
and junk yards gleaming in the brittle metal light of the sun.

She had no use for it, the loneliness of the place,
or for the neighbors with their stubborn religion and stunted children,
so she left it to the sun and measly rain, to the wind's rat-tail file,
cursing the taxes, pocketing the oil money, selling what she could,
the horses in the stable, the contents of the china and linen cabinets,
the silver, the furniture. The ploughs and harrows and other implements,
all older than the century, she left, like the house, to rot,
not bothering to search the barn, its harvest of straw and mold, its huge population
    of mice,
or climb the garrulous stairs to the world beneath the roof.

That pilgrimage falls to us, her children, stung by snow in our rush
from car to house, puffing like engines in the coarse chill,
the damp foetor of decay. For us these neglected heirlooms have waited, their quiet
    tainted
only by the unceasing rasp of derrick, the doppler whine of small airplanes,
a snowmobile or chainsaw, in darkness smelted gold in summer or silvered by the moon,
rats and moths, termites, weevils and silverfish reaping the spoils
of that old prosperity, asking only to be left to trunks of letters and fine lace,
patiently digesting cellulose from forests which have disappeared even in memory.
Sixty rocking chairs we count, the collection mother's memory had numbered in the
    hundreds,
stacked four and five high, angled oddly like Northwest tribal gods,
or tumbled in piles like skyscrapers after a temblor.

What did we expect? A hidden source of wealth?
We flash our lights across the floor and into corners
and witness the noiseless scurrying of predator and prey.
What urges us to find in such small lives some measure of ourselves?
We open a rotten trunk and view shattered layers of ancient plastic
and in-between dust of flax, spoor of silk,
fashioned like snowflakes in unrepeatable radial symmetries
by girls in the old counties, young girls going blind in tallow light,
and in another raddled hulk, packets of letters bound with ribbon
like a young girl's braids, the paper splitting, the script faded and foreign seeming
in its careful elaboration. One speaks of the heat of a distant summer,
and another guardedly alludes to the "recent excitement" which ended
in the elm beside the barn, "the hanging tree."

I remember a story my father said his father told,
how in a place not much further south, twelve men,
guineas like himself—who saved and later owned the fields just like any redneck Baptist—
those *guineas*, black as Africans from working in the fields, apostles of miscegenation,
twelve men tried for a sheriff's murder, were acquitted, and lynched anyway,
because they were . . ., because their beautiful bronze skin made them not quite human.

Why do I think they are calling me with pincer clicks, ticking of claws on wood,
a phantom flickering of wings that dart through twilight into fathomless night?
My breath rises in moist clouds out of the numb light, a lack of feeling in my frozen hands
as I hold these messengers from the past, their skin as transparent as mother's when she was dying.
I am holding the body of the past, what she has become, what we all become.

Needing air, even the blue air outside, I find a tree whose roots have split the barn's foundation,
a giant tree without bark or hint of leaf, humbled years ago by a pest
that, invisible as the Angel of Death, swept across the land—
and from a lower limb a stained, discolored piece of hemp unravels in the wind,
strand by splintered strand. I touch it, bring it close
to my face, try to gauge the color of the stain, pull on it
until I think I will break, until overhead I hear a crack and splitting
and at my feet a sudden crash. When we leave, I turn
and look again, the bloodshot sun sets the ruined grove,
the dying house on fire. Oh, let them live, I pray, who toil
unnoticed by the world. Grant them their share of misery,
and no more. And when their end comes, let it be quick
and merciful as the flight of talons in the ravenous dark.

Anywhere but Mississippi!

I never knew I had ninety cousins,
sons and daughters of the sons and daughters
of the original five, my coevals—

hell, there were great and great-great grandkids
half of them working for FedEx, the only
place to put all those mushrooms—

and me there with wife and one lousy bairn—
fruitful but not multiplicative.
Every day another party—

one day hush puppies and crappie—
since his disability Cousin Sonny (Angelo
on his birth certificate) drifted all year in a dinghy

hauling sunfish out of a lake
stacking the catch in his giant freezer chest
for the family fish fry—

the tiny fish, one or two bites worth,
breaded in milk and corn meal and deep-fried
in lard, bubbling in the vat,

the fryer big as a hot tub—
female and male alike like the souls of the damned—
who could hear their arteries harden above

the din of all those cousins?
Or else it was wine-tasting, someone's friend
the only distributor in town,

this when only the dagoes drank wine—
(nothing but whisky and beer for the "natives")
getting pickled on Brother Timothy's

favorite pinots and cabernets—
it wasn't bad, but once you were loose
there was nothing to talk about—

politics? the coloreds? Either it was football
all day and in any weather, nothing
but tailbacks and Hail Marys, these late-come Volunteers,

flying the Confederate battle flag of football—
or else the "in" they had with the Sheriff—
how many of them had how many tickets

from the zealous constabulary—
driving while Italian—"fixed"—
how many neutered dagoes at that table?

Or else it was a stunned and drunken viewing,
a religious ritual really,
the *Godfather* saga, ten hours starting

at ten in the morning and ending as we adjourned
for creamed corn, creamed spinach,
biscuits, gravy, some bloody roast,

pie then and ice cream, topped with more alcohol—
some yellow stuff in a tall phallic bottle
(distilled urine samples from

Sicilian and Calabrian refugees)
or else we returned to the TV, Marlon Brando,
our Christ-figure, our sacrificial mumbler

filling the giant screen with his overheated cheeks,
the baby creeping along the hearth
ledge, teetering over a marble abyss.

Crapheads

Did you see Nancy's dress, the one
she wore at the inaugural, the red one?
That was mine. My ladies do the best
bead work on the West Coast. All

the producers' wives love my gowns.
People look at the beads, the sequins,
not at the loose skin under those chins.
My business is all word of mouth.

What was I talking about?
Oh, my sister-in-law. I like to say
Southerners are the nicest people
in the world—even if they'd condemn you

to hell, they'll smile and you'll never know.
(I do it too, don't I, Robert?) My sister-in-law,
she was always such a cute thing.
Still keeps a lovely house. Course,

she's got help. Ruby's been with her,
must be thirty years or more!
But she's got good taste
for a girl that only went to secretarial school.

She and my brother have the biggest collection
of opera recordings in the whole Memphis area code.
Whenever we visit, they stack those damn '78's
on the player high as the ceiling.

(I exaggerate, of course. Robert can tell you,
can't you, Robert. Okay, they're not '78's anymore.)
Morning till night, all those Dago bitches
shrieking about some craphead done 'em wrong.

Of course, he done 'em wrong.
All those Dago crapheads
are the same. 'Cept for me.
I'm too nice to be a craphead.

Found that out in the Navy.
The other guys, all they wanted from shore leave
was a sore wanker. I might have wanted
that too, but you have to be careful

when you're not a craphead.
Me and Robert, my sister-in-law
calls him my partner—ho! ho! ho!,
as Santa might say—me and Robert

been living together for,
what is it now, Robert honey,
twenty-four, twenty-five years?
Whenever we go to Memphis,

my sister-in-law insists on putting
us up, me in one bedroom and Robert
in another. No sneaking around
like they do in some *opera buffa*,

she can hear a mouse sneeze
in that giant house of hers.
I talked to my brother, I said, *Frank,
this has got to stop.*

*You know and I know that Robert
is a heckuva lot more to me
than a partner.* But Frank, he's a fine one
for domestic tranquility, he says

to humor her. So we get to the table—
and I have to say that Ruby knows pork fat
like I know beads—me on one side, Robert on the other,
like Romeo and Juliet and that goddam wall,

and my sister-in-law is nattering away
about which opera companies are comin'
to Memphis, and how her little Bianca
is the belle of the kiddie ballet—

jus' between you and me, that child
is never gonna be any kind of ballet
dancer, for one thing she moves
like one of those Disney hippos with

hip dysplasia and for another she's
the hairiest thing you ever seen
outside the zoo—until she gets
to the point of the whole charade.

If I had a nickel for every time
she asked me who I'm datin'
and why I'm not married, I'd be
even richer than I already am.

I suppose in Memphis you can
make ball gowns for rich old ladies
and still be a craphead, but in Hollywood,
darlin', it helps to be something else.

Pastures

We come with the dust and we go with the wind

    — *Woody Guthrie*

A friend calls to say she's been in the hospital
    again,
    not just the E.R., but intensive care,

her blood pressure erratic as the stock market.
    It's been raining
    there, mudslides and flash floods sweeping

household pets into canyons. At least, she's still got her view of
    the Pacific,
    even if she's not enjoying it like she used to.

Up here, I tell her, the lawns are drying out,
    sunburnt
    like an old man's skull—

the hottest year on record, two years
    in a row.
    "How long can we keep the string alive," the sportscaster

jokes with the weatherman. GPS won't help us navigate
    the Anthropocene—
    terrible name for this terrible new age.

We see it coming on the Weather Channel—windstorm,
    firestorm,
    deluge—but refuse to do anything that might

make our lives less comfortable. Thank you,
    say the forests,
raining ash and cinders on suburban roofs.

Thank you, say the streambeds, charting
    the dried
    arteries of the past. Our dog, a rescue

pet, has the whole back yard, brown and dusty
    as himself,
    to shit in. We've loved and cared for

him like the finest pure bred, but he's
    damaged goods,
    barks at every leaf blower and garbage man,
bites friends and strangers without distinction,
    shivers
    when our daughter howls with headache

or anxiety. Last week someone in our church
    lost her son,
    twenty-one and with a history

of drugs and alcohol. His girlfriend found him
    in bed, unconscious.
    He never woke up. Was it drugs? Alcohol?

Nobody will say. All they'll say is what a bright
    spirit he was,
    how creative, filled with life.

And now it's gone, nobody's fault. At least
    nobody's
    taking the blame.

Rockets' Red Glare

Finally, the heat is here, and those insipid partisans of spring,
the pansies, are wilting under the sun's long-delayed stare.
A melted cat lazes serpentine on the sidewalk.
Gold leaf is cracking on the beatific domes of mushrooms.
Jets hammer the skies like distant thunder,
and the doves, those incorrigible nesters,
have finally moved on, now their kids are grown,
not yet eaten by neighborhood cats.
They're summering in the magnolia's high branches,
proclaiming undying love in the hazy swelter.

The bougainvillea, exotic weed born to the smelter,
sheds a thousand crimson butterflies and grows a thousand more
as I trudge through desert heat content with my loneliness.
The neighbors are all at grandma's eating cherries and steak.
Only their dogs know someone is loose in the neighborhood.
Out on the boulevard cars pass like surf bullying the shore.
But here I can walk in the middle of the street where shade is thickest.
From behind a fence a Boxer tells me that the street belongs to him.
I bless his warning, taking as my model St. Francis
who threw away his wealth so he could talk pigeon.

The trees, Siberian elms, line the street, tall, graceful as ballerinas,
whispering their surprise at finding themselves in the desert.
So much thermal energy, they want to shout,
but all those Russian winters have taught them restraint.
Tonight, a forest of fire and smoke will blossom overhead
and children will lift gilded faces skyward,
their little houses still lonely and waiting for someone to return.
For a few minutes maybe I'll go out on my porch,
zealot of the holy and the wholly useless, and with the trees
quiver convivially at the brilliant, bloodthirsty show.

LUCKY STIFF

Courtship consists in a number of quiet attentions, not so pointed as to alarm, nor so vague as not to be understood.

— Laurence Sterne

*oh god it's wonderful
to get out of bed
and drink too much coffee
and smoke too many cigarettes
and love you so much.*

— Frank O'Hara

The Aerialist

She wears her shrink-wrap skin like Venus
wears her toga, revealing, not concealing
the pure marble of her muscles.
For two acts she tantalizes,
seated on her tiny garlanded swing,
with fawn-like looks and legs
chiseled by the daily conquest of gravity,
this not quite human girl
who seems all hydraulics
and tubular steel. I wonder
at the will that produces such compact
concentration. Even her breasts
are miracles of compact concentration.

Perhaps the gods adore her too.
I can almost feel their jealousy,
as finally in act three she throws
herself on air and soars
so close to their realm, this Icarus
who has pared her body
until it lifts like an aileron
in the breath of our attention.

How can they face their own desire?
Is that what makes them gods,
the knowledge that immolated
in the fire of the moment,
they will somehow survive
to suffer the next?

Who else can face that blaze?
And yet we try, faces upturned,
dazzled by the spotlight
as she grips the rings with one foot,
spreading her arms to receive
our embrace. We give her wings,
who fear for her, who ache
at her ascension. Too late

the memory of our roots, buried
safely in the ground—
the quickening in our skin,
the knot in our groins.

Gare Saint-Lazare

We've both seen the postcard in museum gift shops,
two trains wreathed in smoke, dark figures
swirling between, almost smoke themselves,
the roof resting on nothing but air.

Behind the trains you see three more car-barns—foreshortened,
gothic—and a tall building as weightless as the sky.
And the sky, blue-grey like the steam floating above the trains.
Everything volatile, gaseous, about to evanesce.

When I think of the train station
in Madrid, not the Atocha, but the smaller one
to the north, this is what I see, hopelessly
romanticized and out of date. All the pain

of leaving you made pretty and whole.
Everything in flight, even me. Even you.

Foil

I ride the long arc of the freeway
through West L.A., the low, bland shops
and houses flexing in the heat like mats
of algae, distant hills and towers
wrapped in petrochemical gauze. I'm
thinking about love the way fishermen
on the pier must think about their tropical homes,
the shacks and shanties filled with children,
the carbide-tainted waters teeming with fish
every color of metal. Has the pollution
of their dreams been slow or quick?
I catch the glare off a taller building,
that hospital, and am nearly blinded
by the memory of a girl's copper hair.

Liebestoadstool

It was almost religion. Word would spread
from friend to neighbor, from neighbor to kin
and soon the woods would ring with the rattle

of pails, with children and families, singles
and couples in boots scouring the green
October gloom, the marshy undergrowth,

for any kind of fungus. You were there
with another man's wife, almost a couple
yourselves. What were you seeking,

the two of you? You had no idea what
she wanted aside from the clamor
of sex. Was that all you wanted from this

dour, self-questioning woman, the two
of you as well-matched as a pair of
hand-wrought, amateur candelabra?

What glimmered then between you,
wax dripping along the candle, along
the slumped, imperfect glaze, pooling

on the table where you ate? Your eyes
were no match for the woman's,
morels and chanterelles outwitting you

with their G.I. (genetic issue) camo,
dusky umbrellas and spongiform cones
all in khaki and taupe, they knew how

to hide from your hungers, clumsy
and self-absorbed. But not hers.
Back at her apartment, you lingered

at the window, sipping something tart
as vinegar while the patchwork of wood
and high-rise receded into dusk.

You listened as she toiled in the kitchen,
the smell of onions and underbrush
wafting like some meal out of a fairy tale.

What about her husband? When would
he be home? You never thought of him
except when you were with her.

Suddenly you were struck with fantasy,
the brown oleaginous blobs simmering
in the pan were Death Cap and, like a witch

in a *Märchen*, who only seemed beautiful,
she was fixing your last meal. He'd arrive
and find the two of you stricken at the table.

Who knew she was capable of such vengeance?
Who knew you were so riddled with guilt?

April's Fool

I'm driving up the 101 in a U-Haul stepvan,
stepchild of my own marriage. It's 1990.
I've never seen the hills this green. Wild mustard
covers the hills, its yellow antimacassars
reminding me of nature's boundless zest
for repeating itself. In the back my wife's clothes,
half our dishes and pans. She's somewhere
up ahead in a sleek over-priced sports car.

Surprisingly the radio works. "Reach out,
touch faith." I fight it, but a wave of gothic
melancholy washes over me. Once she's settled,
maybe I'll join her. We both know I'm stuck.
We both know she's the one who leaves.

Husbands never do well in fiction.
Charles Bovary. Dagwood Bumstead.
Once we cease being lovers, we become jailers.
Poor Blondie, her abundant golden hair
piled primly, an inverted goblet, on her head,
her beautiful ankles and calves unnoticed
by her browbeaten, dithering spouse.
How she must long to unpin those thick
tresses and let them fall on that swan's neck,
those pale shoulders. How she must long
for some stronger arm to pull a brush
through the golden fleece, static leaping
in those billowing clouds like lightning.

I took my ice princess to the hills and set her
free. Now I am the desert, parched
and teeming with whatever refuses to die.

Horizon Event

That winter I wore two sweaters
and an extra roll of fat—
the life belt that kept me afloat
in a featureless, sucking ocean.

Up the horizon came the reggae
of party ships. "Read this," friends
called from the brightly-colored decks,
brightly-colored books chunking divots

from my scalp and shoulders.
Self-loathing, self-love,
I was capable of neither.
A new scripture was being written

and a new Jerusalem peopled
with the happily self-satisfied.
I wanted to shout,
"I deserve to suffer,"

who had never known anything
but self-inflicted pain.
Nemesis, that friendly goddess
came dressed like a distant relative

holding store-bought flowers
as for a hospital visit.
We danced, I was on deck now,
a tenement deflecting the wrecking

ball's insistent hand.
And yet I wanted the collapse,
a pile of rubble
secret as a tomb.

The angel laughed, the dark
goddess brighter now
than morning, and dragged me
from my bed. "Look at that,"

she whispered, lovers
touching hands and hair.
"They do not deserve this
happiness, but it is theirs."

When Jesus invited the cripple to
carry the burden of his stretcher,
how long was he grateful?
I'll bet it was hot in Palestine

and the crowd of well-wishers
had run off after Jesus,
hungry for the next magic show.
And what about the bearers,

suddenly unemployed?
Or poor dead Lazarus
stepping from the cool of his crypt
into the glare of public regard?

Did he ever wash the stench
from his raddled skin
or comprehend his sister's sadness
at her sudden loss of freedom?

It's been three years since you left
and still my nerves are tangled
in the body's wiring cabinet,
neurons firing like accidental cannons

in autonomic night. I am saved,
cast on shore with the other refugees
from love. No surprise that some of us
swim past the reef and lose ourselves in the depths.

Every so often I look to the horizon
and notice a cloud sailing like a comma
at the edge of sight.
Is that your ship? Returning?

Lip Service

Our little crowd of smokers huddle under the awning
outside the Tattle Tale Room, our Abel's offering
of sin tax and tobacco rising into the drenched
and chilly air. At the other end of the parking lot,
beyond Big Lou's Toys & Collectibles, the Aquarium,
the Korean cleaners and Kamikaze Comics,
the partisans of the Scarlet Lady are swapping
lights and jokes, before returning to the serious
business of pouring a lifetime's sorrows
down the hair-clogged drain of their neighbor's ear.

My ex is there, I'll bet, and her new beau,
a beefy former-cop-turned-security-consultant—
I think his name is Jeff. They'd be laughing by now,
and she'd be telling him for the 33rd time all the ways
I failed her. She likes to tell the story of her life,
each boyfriend or husband forming a chapter,
all of them starting with lust or jealousy
and ending in disaster. I've heard earlier
versions dozens of times. And even the latest
more times than I'd care to count,
the last time in court. She's good at getting
people, even judges, to feel sorry for her.
I did, even though I had my own tale of woe,
which I shared like a wandering minstrel
with whoever would listen. At least I used to.

I used to think I was self-destructive
because of what dad did to mom,
or what mom did to me, but now I know
that I like booze and cigarettes not just because they help
me forget. Standing in the rain with the other hardy
hackers, I enjoy watching our puffy, red faces
bobbing like balloons against a backdrop of asphalt and rain.
It gives us a reason to be here, in the cold and wet,
while dads with takeout and kids holding baggies
filled with goldfish scurry like roaches to their cars.

Nothing's better than that last puff when
the nicotine is densest and you can almost feel
the glowing tip sear your lungs,
holding it in as you crush the butt
into a grimy paste and head back into the bar.

Ludus Amatorius (The Sport of Love)*

When you see a girl staring at the wide screen
above the bar, ask her if she prefers the Yankees
or the Mets. If it's Yanks, then you're facing
a long, slow courtship with many expensive gifts,
way beyond your means, or even mine.
If she says Mets, then a couple of dates
at cheap Italian restaurants should find you
in her bed. Or maybe she's ogling basketball.
"Knicks or Nets?" you ask. If it's Knicks,
you're looking at a pricey apartment on the Upper
West Side, private schools for the kids, and a new
Mercedes every Hanukkah. If she answers Nets,
then it's crab cakes at the beach, a moonlit walk
above an oily tide, and then a quickie
in the salt grass. When you're done, don't forget
to enjoy the surf's polite applause and brush
the sand from her naked, chilly bottom.
But if you see a girl screaming at the hockey
game flickering above the corner cash register,
you're in luck. Ask her if she's a Devils fan
and buy her a beer. Buy her another, and get
ready for some contact sport. Don't bring
your pads, just a willingness to give
and take bruises. Be sure to enjoy
ripping the jersey from her torso.
And don't flinch when she body checks you
or readies herself for a slap shot. There's still
the bloody, enthusiastic grappling, pelvis to groin,
across your living room as you kick
the coffee table and knock over a lamp
and she's scoring your back with her jet black
fingernails and you're choking her into
unconsciousness. Pretend you're the puck
screaming towards the goal. No penalties for high
sticking here, stick her anywhere you can,
high, low, front or back, because when you wake,
she'll be gone and you'll be a shattered, happy wreck.

*You're probably aware of Ovid's naughty poem Ars Amatoria (The Art of Love). Some critics say it was this poem which got him banished to the least civilized corner of the Roman Empire. My poem is a small updating of his poem, which except for its callous disregard for conventional morality, was essentially advice to the lovelorn, a how-to manual for boys who were having trouble meeting girls, a sort of Roman Tucker Max.

Nocturne: Crow and Weasel
— *for MS*

All afternoon we lay naked in bed
drinking wine and reading
a children's book to one another,
passing it back & forth like a joint.

Somewhere in our apartment building a TV
blared like the froth & ebb of a storm.
Two boys leave their home in an immense
grass sea. Together they discover forests,

mountains, great rivers and lakes, and people
like themselves, afraid of every stranger.
Wind rattled the bedroom windows,
our voices quavering with glass vibrato.

All summer they travel north
until they come to water so wide
there is no crossing, the bears
great white blocks of ice, the people

so different they forget to be afraid.
Rain pattered like birds flocking on the roof.
And so they returned, and we with them,
having opened the book of wonder,

through snow-drenched passes, bitter valleys,
and rivers of brittle ice, winter passages
and pages of hunger, almost freezing
to death in an ocean of icy grass,

warmth only in the twining
of their own frail bodies.
It doesn't matter who saved them.
God is generous to the young

and quickly shuts the book of suffering.
And then, because we were tired, we made love
and slept in a drift of pillows and sheets,
awaking to darkness and hunger, but lingering

awhile. I caressed her black plumage.
She smoothed my sable fur.
And we listened to the thunder
of closets slamming and closing gates,

as the vastness of our separate lives
opened around us on this,
the last afternoon of childhood.

Naked

I

If you never saw your parents naked
or if you can remember each time,
then you're someone like me,

someone embarrassed to take off
his clothes in front of his own children,
even when camping, even in the close

confines of a tent. In the seminary,
the freshman all slept in a large
L-shaped room, dressing and undressing

in the privacy of our bathrobes.
We called it "modesty,"
a habit I acquired at home,

where the four of us always changed
behind a bathroom or bedroom door,
privacy and shame our closest intimates.

II

—Mount Desert Island, Maine

When you stripped in the woods,
and dove, naked as a naiad, into the chill
green waters of a pond, I could not follow

your example, but waded in my underwear
into the murky shallows, the bottom
clotted with stones and the muck

of my own misgiving. Every step
tested something sharp. Glass?
Tin from careless campers?

Even dazzled by the restless water's
beads of light, dapple or shade,
I could not settle my fear,

and so I swam to the far shore,
with each stroke inhaling chill
mist into heaving lungs.

I guess you forgave me.
I haven't changed, nor have you,
shifting from pajamas to skin to blouse

in full view of our daughter and even
our son. You wait for me, while I hide
in the bathroom, afraid to look

over my shoulder at the blur of white
gathering cloth about its frailty.

III

—Braunschweig, Bundesrepublik Deutschland

After a night of dancing and beer—
an almost endless night, sundown
at three, dawn at midmorning—

we went to the sauna. Not my idea,
and even though it offered a chance
to see the women naked, I had no desire

to let others gaze at me. But still
I went, don't ask me why. I couldn't face
my empty room, or what I'd bring

to that cold and functional space.
I was an asteroid flying through
the vastness of my life,

all interactions at a distance.
It was that or catastrophe, wasn't it?
After showers, we met in a large, warm pool,

staving off drunkenness with the crawl
or breast stroke, the bodies pink and pale,
muscles loose now after the cold.

The sauna next, dry heat sucking
moisture from lips and nose,
and then the hot tub, breasts floating

like aquatic potatoes, penises wagging
like tube worms. By now the beer
had leached from our pores,

and what was left was a warmth,
something like love, and yet we were not
done, but like our Neanderthal elders

we shuffled past a heavy wooden door
and onto the garden porch,
its railing heaped with snow.

It could've been twenty-five or thirty degrees,
but in the glow of our common bravery,
we forgot the cold and listened

to the silence gathered placidly above us,
snow sifting out of the dark
like sugar onto shoulders and hair.

Kumquat

I give you only this, Love,
its pith of strings,
seeds and cloying juice,
the ugly squawking sounds.

When I was younger,
there was so much more,
fruit that glowed dimly
in the leaves of the future.

If only you could have tasted
that river, all the flavors
of sky and petal
rushing into your mouth!

You would've felt among the chosen.
Or so I tell myself,
who now must win you
with this small coin,

whose truth must be tested
with the teeth and swallowed
in a bite, the bitter and the sweet
mingling on the tongue.

Undergrowth

When Br'er Fox tossed the Rabbit
into a dense tangle of thorn,
he was doing what we all do,
condemning others as we'd
condemn ourselves.
If he had spent his youth
among the canes,
he'd have known
how companionable those
narrow halls can be.
I think about the women
on my computer screen—
their hillocks clear-cut—
and women I've known,
their genital fuzz or fluff
downy as dust bunnies,
and then consider my luck
in finding you, adorned
with sprigs of tough
wiry hair, a dark halo
surrounding each nipple,
and the insistent scribble
from navel to nest,
where only the most
delicate coaxing—
tongue chafed and
littered with thicket—
reveals what the fox
could only dream, a secret
passage, the way through.

A Tour of Scotland: An Epithalamium

Gathered in a double-wide up a dry arroyo,
four men survey a copse of golden bottles—
my bachelor party, number three.
My new brothers welcome me
according to the customs of their clan.
Tonight is special, nothing blended—
a hurried glimpse from a jumbo jet—
we're crossing that narrow Northern land
on foot—one still moment, then the next,
starting in the heights, the air chill
and dense with mist, the liquor
molten caramel, sharp as flint,
Dalwhinnie to Glenmorangie,
a wee cup at each stop,
savoring the ascetic pleasures
of the moor, a breath of heather,
then something like milk wrung from granite.
Although it is invisible to our clouded sight,
we can smell the distant sea.
Slowly we work downhill,
Bladnoch and Glenkinchie,
a whiff of berry and oak,
the eternal, o'ermastering bite
of the sea. What we celebrate is
as fragrant, as difficult to hold
as the brute sea wind—a future
with their sister, my betrothed.
The squash of toe and heel
echoes in our bones, each thimble
a torch warming some unknown knot
of wariness and rage as we venture
in our wherry from island to isle,
Highland Park, Tobermory, and Talisker,
each smoky sip of peat, urine clear
and bright as brine. The daughter
of the house waits with sisters
and friends, tense with the mystery
of dishevelment, the body's ache
and rapture, what tomorrow brings.

Confessions of a Lapsed Gym Rat

Children, once I was not as you see me now,
not the stumbling, confused mumbler
who questions your every action and word.
"What? Did you say something? What was that
you said?" Up every morning before six
I worked the circuit—lats and abs, delts and tri's and bi's—
climbed the stairs, rode the bike,
and then an hour stepping up & over,
down & around the plastic double step.
We were beautiful
in our spandex and sweat-stained lycra,
hair pulled back or caught in bands
of terry cloth, eyes bright with exertion,
muscles taut and gleaming. It was a dance
whose only goal was the glow
which surrounded us
in the locker room and on the drive to work.
Cast us in bronze, carve us in marble,
we were that close to ideal.
And still we never stopped,
knowing that if we ever renounced
our zeal, if ever we fell
from perfection's path
and strayed into love's byways,
into preschools and maternity wards,
we'd be shut from those bright Edenic doors,
musclebound angels standing guard,
condemned to pass the display windows,
others now striding purposefully toward the unattainable,
while we trudged by,
exhausted and pudgy and faithful to something less
elusive, something other than ourselves.

Dinner with the Cannibal

Standing imperiously in her highchair,
my two-year-old reaches with her fork
and jabs my arm. "I eat you up, Daddy,"
she tells me, and I get her point
as she stabs me again in the ear.
"I eat Daddy head," she declares gleefully
popping the tines between ruddy baby lips,
and I remember reading about New Guinea
hill people, how they eat dead relatives,
scooping the curded pudding of the brain
from its china cup, growing sick from the feast.
How long before my own gray
matter begins to mimic Sponge Bob?
I should warn her about the dangers
of spooning up the past, what she might find
on her trip through Ireland and Italy
back beyond Australopithecus
to the Great Mother of us all. This Eucharist,
the sacrament of family, has perils for the stoutest
heroine. No matter. Armed with shining
fork, she's fearless. Insatiable historian,
she'll devour it all, welcome the fullness,
and maybe then take time to wonder what it means.

Forty

It takes forty days, say students of human behavior,
to form new habits, a daily exercise routine, say.
Less than that, we're more than likely to quit,
but more, inertia and a sense of inevitability

take over. Who can remember what they were doing
a month and a half ago? Surely it was the same thing
we did yesterday, or last week, that thing we can't
stop doing. I'm staring at my glass of wine,

one of my favorite wines, and it's staring back.
We are about to part company for forty days—
Ash Wednesday to Easter—neither of us knowing
if we'll ever share the other's good graces again.

"I'm sorry," I want to say, "You've been such a good
friend, seeing me through highs and lows, but
especially lows, and now . . . well, now, I'm on
a new high, at least I hope to be." Wasn't that the point

of Buddha's forty days under the bodhi tree,
wild dogs and centipedes and his own restless self?
Or Jesus in the desert? Who was that devil anyway—
the Devil himself, or some understudy, some trainee

unable to close the deal? If only it were as simple
as Jonah, three days in the belly of some kind of whale—
probably not a gray whale or the ones you see
in Pacific Life commercials, more like Monstro,

an Ahab-devouring sperm. It took forty days and forty
nights of gully-washing to cleanse the Old World,
cities and people, farms and animals,
all that lost DNA. And Ali Baba couldn't get by with less

than forty thieves. One person, one habit, forty days,
but think about a people, how it took the Israelites
forty years to get over their Egyptian habits, Thoth & Isis,
before they were ready to enter into the land of the New God.

Me, I'm too fond of Dry Gewürztraminer. Will I be a better
person if I give it up? Will something new and better
come into my life? The last time I tried to give up wine,
I developed a taste for craft-brewed whiskey, and when

I gave up whiskey, it was for heirloom marijuana.
What I can't give up is that sense of starting fresh,
the feeling that I've just slid out of my mother's womb
and that all of life waits for me now I've been delivered.

A Field

Yesterday, four-year-old daughter in hand,
I slalomed the farmers market, crowds
of vegans, retirees, and trophy wives reaching parsley

and pomelos to vendors at their battered scales.
Espresso smell mingled with rotting vegetables.
We stopped for a trio of teenagers banging out cool jazz,

the two of us stones in a creek surging with spring flood.
And as we stood there, I felt myself receding, three decades,
to Nüremberg, the *Christkindlmarkt*, shoppers thronging stalls

of ornaments and cheap East-bloc toys (a giant goose-stepping
Nutcracker guarded the tree towering in the middle of the *Platz*).
Thirty years earlier the city, its half-timbered houses draped

with swastikas, had hosted the biggest shindig of the thousand-year *Reich*.
The woman I was with, I'd known her just a few weeks.
Like opposing armies, we'd been exhaustively mapping

each other's bodies. She had a limp—an early skirmish
with polio. Too weak to sustain a frontal assault,
she was in constant retreat, forcing me to attack

her flank or thrust from the rear. That was just between us.
To everyone else we looked smitten as new mittens,
holding hands, stuffing the other's cheeks with *Wiener Mandeln*.

Now we were out in the open, cool November on our lips.
We passed sugar beets heaped like cannon balls waiting
for the French attack. The field rose in corduroy welts

to a ridge where we could view the folded Hessian landscape
like Field Marshals on maneuvers. I tried to imagine the armies,
the millions of dead, but kept coming back to my own

unhappiness, other women I'd known,
my paltry triumphs of will, *the little Führer*.
I hadn't thought of that sleeping field for years,

or the woman, who slipped from my life as easily as one day
lapses into the next. But last night as I lay in bed with wife
and child, I saw it again, more real than their warm,

breathing bodies, saw it littered with autumn and our shadows
twining as we climbed. The sun at our backs caressed a last distant
hilltop, and then we stepped into darkness and numbing cold.

Family Tree

Once in our twenties we thought we would never die.

   — Elizabeth Spires

I watch my son high in the magnolia
where branches thin. His sister
at the foot of the tree shrieks for him

to come down and play with her. They know I am
watching, that I will catch him when he falls
and save her from loneliness.

They know I will be watching even when
I have sunk into the ground like the water
I sprinkle on lilies and grapes.

How they know this I do not know,
just as I don't know where my son learned
to trust the net of leaf and limb

that keeps him aloft or what bird
gave my daughter her heartbreaking cries.
If only they could see what I see,

their father rising slowly into air,
becoming that mix of sunshine and vapor,
a brightness that brings them to tears.

Hallein Above Salzburg

Jesus tomb or mouth of hell—
what was I thinking as I steered

my little family into salt mine #1
high in the Austrian Alps?

We'd tried so many roles in our tour
of that vast pan-German theme park—

all those castles and museums—
yeoman bowman, miniature knight,

cleric, peasant, merchant, inquisitor.
What costume should we wear next?

I know, let's play prisoner
chipping halite from the rocks

breathing salt dust until our lips
and lungs are beef jerky.

Perhaps if we walk far enough,
we'll meet those two Italians,

the Mantuan and the Florentine
coming back from their own expedition

into terror. The town bought its wealth
here with the lives of miners—

built its fortress, paid its soldiers.
"Salary" comes from the word 'sal,'

Latin for salt. We take a wooden slide
screaming from one level to the next,

ride a boat across the River of Forgetting,
River of No Return, part of it in Austria,

part in hell—the salt runs like a river
and the miners followed it

like hunters after rabbit or elk.
What did they want that you and I

don't want? How soon did they
abandon hope? In Amsterdam

the poor were housed in rooms
that flooded when they worked

too slowly, death by drowning
or pneumonia. And off the coast

of Lampedusa the boats, too full
of people, take on water,

sea water, filled with salt
once worth its weight in gold.

Why do human lives still weigh
so much less? When we return,

we'll pack this foreign substance
in our luggage, astringent, bitter,

without which nothing tastes sweet.

Wasserspiele

Schloß Hellbrunn, Salzburg

It's said that the Prince Archbishop of Salzburg,
after meditating on poverty
and the limits of power,
built this palace, prototype
for all future Playboy Mansions.
The walls of the *Kronengrotte,* for instance,
illustrate the Baroque at its most
playful, a mix of classical fragment—
gilded of course—and shell mosaics.
In the center of the foyer
a golden crown rises and falls
on a jet of water, demonstrating
to the prince and his friends
the wisdom their Latin teachers
had beaten into their gold and copper
heads, *mutatis mutandis.* Meanwhile
in the back room a blond hero
presses a knife to a satyr's throat.
The satyr is tied to the trunk
of a dwarf fig tree, its clustered
leaves conveniently hiding his sex
from the archbishop's guests.
As they leave, water squirts
their legs and skirts, and arches
above them as they rush away
only to be doused by more spray,
its machine-gun spurt and stutter
planned and paid for by the sly,
fun-loving prelate.
Here on a hot summer's day
we tourists protect our phones
and cameras from the foretold yet
unexpected splash, wondering if the shower
masters of Belsen and Dachau
had also spent a pleasant hour
here watching as drenched
families huddled and shrieked.

Draining the Lake

Like pilgrims visiting the tombs of saints,
smoky hands of angels on our shoulders,
we wandered the medieval city, stone churches
and tall half-timbered houses leaning over
narrow streets. After lunch, we walked to a nature
preserve where we used to meet twenty years before.

Or maybe the only pilgrim was me,
having flown a night and a day to visit
my memories. She'd lived here her whole life,
one day's dust settling on every yesterday,
whereas for me that brief, vivid time was fresh
as photos in an acid-free album.

I remembered her, still almost a girl,
lithe as exposed wire, electrons ready to jump
into my hand and burn through my body.
Who had she become, who once was so hungry for love?

All around us the short bright summer
was having its way with things. In dappled shade
we walked beside the three lakes at the center
of the preserve. From the air, they might have looked
like the chambers of a heart, pumping the valley's
blood into the river which surrounded the town
like a moat. The ducks, not so wild
that they hadn't grown used to handouts,
guided their little families in tight formation,
like convoys on the lookout for U-boats.

In my country, they might be dragging the water
for the body of a gangbanger, or else one of the lakes
would be drained and workmen in waders and gas masks
would be collecting milk cartons, beer bottles,
old tires, and a mountain of plastic wrappers.
Here they don't throw trash in the lakes—
at least they pretend they don't.
Here they let bodies sink into the mud

where the worms can do their work.
I could almost see myself on the bottom of the lake,
slowly decomposing, but alert enough
to notice the oddly matched couple staring
at the surface. Maybe we'd always been wrong
for one another. How could anyone understand
my habit of going in the wrong direction?

I seemed immune to the usual sorts of happiness.
I seemed to thrive on mistakes.
How else explain how happy I'd become?

Seahorse in Saw Grass

it's not his fault he's a lousy swimmer
and must cling to a stalk
or mangrove tangle

does she remember his struggles
with other males
head thrust and tug of war

or that first dance
when she gripped
the same strand of grass

with her tail and they wheeled
in unison as overhead
the water brightened

how willingly he opened
the cleft in his body
head tilted high

the children's rocking
horse, fierce mother,
tender father

and does he remember when
from dawn to dusk
they let go of every anchor

drifted upward
snout to snout
spiraling as they rose

how he seemed to lose
every bearing but her
spinning in that helical

duet toward the world's
shimmering limit
every fourteen days now

she shudders her eggs
into his pouch
slimming as he swells

and all day like a vacuum
he siphons shrimp
and tiny fish

a hovercraft
his gossamer fins'
hummingbird flutter

each morning
she greets him anew
changing color maybe

and leading him in a whirl
around the fronds
until finally tail in tail

they promenade
like an old married couple
walking silently in half light

Orion and the Dipper
gleaming like plankton

Amandatory

I met Amanda sketching a panda at the National Zoo. It was a bitter cold morning, colder than it ever gets in the mountains of China, where the panda's ancestors lived, but the panda seemed happy enough, chewing bright green bamboo grown especially for her somewhere beyond the capital's sprawling suburbs and rushed to the zoo. If the panda had any idea of the immense effort spent on keeping her alive, she would've dropped dead of shame. Amanda was so absorbed in her drawing that she didn't notice me admiring it. It was the living panda, that was clear, but cobbled together from other images—a long-distance tractor trailer, nuclear power stations, storefronts and national monuments creating a panda mosaic whose form and texture was pure panda. Amanda herself, I now saw, was similarly composed of disparate elements: liquid aspirin, hair dye, tooth-whitening gel and thousands of other products the panda's grandparents had never imagined. But then so was I. "A remarkable unlikeness," I said breaking the ice, warm air rushing from my mouth. She looked up, looked at me, then back at the drawing as if trying to incorporate what I had just said into it. "Would you like me to do your portrait?" she asked. The rest, as they say, is story.

About The Author

Lee Rossi was born in St. Louis, Missouri. He studied 5 years for the Roman Catholic priesthood before leaving the seminary. He is the author of three books of poetry, *Wheelchair Samurai* (Plain View Press, 2012), *Ghost Diary* (Terrapin Press, 2003) and *Beyond Rescue* (Bombshelter Press, 1992), and has appeared in various anthologies, including *Don't Leave Hungry: 50 Years of the Southern Poetry Review* (The University of Arkansas Press, 2009) and *The Mysterious Life of the Heart* (The Sun Publishing Co., 2009).

His poems, reviews and interviews have been published widely, in *The Southern Review, Tar River Poetry, The Atlanta Review, The Green Mountains Review, The Sun, Poetry East, Chelsea, The Wormwood Review, Nimrod, Beloit Poetry Journal, Poet Lore, The Southwest Review* and *The Southern Poetry Review*. He is Staff Reviewer for *Pedestal* and a contributing editor for *Poetry Flash*.

He lives in Northern California.

Acknowledgements

Grateful acknowledgement is made to the editors of the following journals in which some of these poems have previously appeared:

American Poetry Journal: "April's Fool"
Arroyo Literary Magazine: "Lip Service"
Blue Unicorn: "Spraying for Pests"
Cairn: "Taps"
Chariton Review: "An Attic in Downstate Illinois," "Naked" (Parts 2 & 3), "Amandatory"
Clackamas Literary Review: "Horizon Event," "Nocturne: Crow and Weasel"
Culture Weekly: "Pastures" (Winner of the Jack Grapes Poetry Prize)
Main Street Rag: "Missouri Roll"
Miramar: "Stoicism for the Masses"
New Madrid Review: "*Wasserspiele*"
New Mexico Poetry Review: "Foil"
Nimrod: "A Tour of Scotland," "A Field"
Pacific Review: "Mother Tongue"
Poet Lore: "Clinkers," "Knucks," "To the Blackout of '69," "What a Bringdown," "Kumquat," "Naked" (Part 1)
Poetry Northwest: "Gare St-Lazare"
The Porter Gulch Review: "The Sport of Love"
Spillway: "Dinner with the Cannibal"
The Southern Review: "Forty"
The Sun: "A Habit of Ascent," "Sudden Harvest," "Family Tree," "Draining the Lake"
Times Times 3: "Increase + Multiply"
The Tule Review: "Confessions of a Lapsed Gym Rat"
Valparaiso Poetry Review: "Lasting Things"
Willow Glen Poetry Project: "Undergrowth"

Thank You

First off, I would like to thank this collection's early readers, Peter Neil Carroll, Beth Nelson, and Diane Schenker for their help in shaping the book. Their thoughtful and incisive comments helped me clarify my intentions in the various sections as well as in the overall arc of the book.

I would also like to thank the poets in my current workshop, for their inspiration, suggestions and support: Peter Neil Carroll, Esther Kamkar, Anne Cheilek, Terry Adams, Mary Bailey, and Lisa Rizzo. Some of these poems had their beginnings while I still lived in Los Angeles—a shoutout then to my Southern California workshop pals: Florence Weinberger, Sherman Pearl, Nels Christianson, Ellen Reich, Steve Gross, Linda Neal, Terri Niccum, Henry Morro, and Carine Topal.

Thanks also to my various teachers and mentors over the years, especially Jack Grapes and Peter Levitt.

And last but far from least, immense gratitude to my adorable, long-suffering wife, who has had to share me with the Muse from the very beginning of our relationship 23 years ago.

Patrons

Moon Tide Press would like to thank the following people for their support in helping publish the finest poetry from the Southern California region. To sign up as a patron, visit www.moontidepress.com or send an email to publisher@moontidepress.com.

Anonymous
Robin Axworthy
Conner Brenner
Bill Cushing
Susan Davis
Peggy Dobreer
Dennis Gowans
Half Off Books
Jim & Vicky Hoggatt
Ron Koertge & Bianca Richards
Ray & Christi Lacoste
Zachary & Tammy Locklin
Lincoln McElwee
David McIntire
José Enrique Medina
Andrew November
Michael Miller & Rachanee Srisavasdi
Terri Niccum
Ronny & Richard Morago
Jennifer Smith
Andrew Turner
Mariano Zaro

Also Available From Moon Tide Press

Dark Ink: A Poetry Anthology Inspired by Horror (2018)
Drop and Dazzle, Peggy Dobreer (2018)
Junkie Wife, Alexis Rhone Fancher (2018)
The Moon, My Lover, My Mother, & the Dog, Daniel McGinn (2018)
Lullaby of Teeth: An Anthology of Southern California Poetry (2017)
Angels in Seven, Michael Miller (2016)
A Likely Story, Robbi Nester (2014)
Embers on the Stairs, Ruth Bavetta (2014)
The Green of Sunset, John Brantingham (2013)
The Savagery of Bone, Timothy Matthew Perez (2013)
The Silence of Doorways, Sharon Venezio (2013)
Cosmos: An Anthology of Southern California Poetry (2012)
Straws and Shadows, Irena Praitis (2012)
In the Lake of Your Bones, Peggy Dobreer (2012)
I Was Building Up to Something, Susan Davis (2011)
Hopeless Cases, Michael Kramer (2011)
One World, Gail Newman (2011)
What We Ache For, Eric Morago (2010)
Now and Then, Lee Mallory (2009)
Pop Art: An Anthology of Southern California Poetry (2010)
In the Heaven of Never Before, Carine Topal (2008)
A Wild Region, Kate Buckley (2008)
Carving in Bone: An Anthology of Orange County Poetry (2007)
Kindness from a Dark God, Ben Trigg (2007)
A Thin Strands of Lights, Ricki Mandeville (2006)
Sleepyhead Assassins, Mindy Nettifee (2006)
Tide Pools: An Anthology of Orange County Poetry (2006)
Lost American Nights: Lyrics & Poems, Michael Ubaldini (2006)

www.ingramcontent.com/pod-product-compliance
Lightning Source LLC
Chambersburg PA
CBHW030813090426
42736CB00027B/621